To:

Pushed Into My Purpose

How God moved me from fear to VICTORY!

God Bless
You Monk.
Always Allow
God to use
you anyway
He sees fit!

Pushed Into My Purpose

How God moved me from fear to VICTORY!

Wanda L. Childs

ISBN: 978-0-9797700-0-5
ISBN: 0-9797700-0-9
Library of Congress Control Number: 2007906625

Additional copies can be ordered at
www.PushedIntoMyPurpose.com
www.blessed247.com

or write to us at

Pushed Into My Purpose
12138 Central Avenue – Suite 387
Mitchellville, MD 20721-1932
Attn: Wanda L. Childs

We would love to get your feedback,
please send emails to info@blessed247.com

Printed in the United States of America

DEDICATION

I dedicate this book to my mother Gladys and my father Edmond, thank you for bringing me into this world and for loving me so much. Mom, you have believed in me from the very beginning, and I love you for your continuous support and encouragement.

I also dedicate this book to my brothers Rik and Jr., who saw the passion in my eyes and determination in my walk. Thank you Rik for all those great ideas, and thank you both for being proud of me. To my only son, I thank you for your patience and understanding while I spent sleepless nights and weekends preparing for this moment. Church on Sunday's was our special time, and I thank God for it.

To the rest of my family and friends, thank you all for allowing me to share all those Blessed 24:7 emails with you.

TABLE OF CONTENTS

Introduction ix

Chapter 1 What has God called you to do? 1

Chapter 2 Trusting God in the Middle of the Storm... 5

Chapter 3 The Faith Walk—Where is Your Faith? 9

Chapter 4 When Friends and Family Abandon You.... 13

Chapter 5 Taking Inventory of the Company You Are Keeping—Getting Rid of the Dream Killers... 17

Chapter 6 Is That You God? Because Sometimes Satan Tries To Get a Word In... 21

Chapter 7 Pushed into My Purpose—Moving from Fear to Victory... 25

Chapter 8 Pursuing Your Dreams 29

INTRODUCTION

The purpose of this book is to share my heartfelt testimony with you in hopes that it will encourage and motivate you to be obedient when God calls you to your purpose. Often we are not walking in our purpose, and we miss our blessings because of fear and lack of faith. Just know whatever God has for you it is for you and no one can take that away.

When God calls you into your purpose, do not allow fear to block your blessings. Trust the promise of God and remember, if God called you, He will make sure you lack nothing for your journey.

As I share with you some of the storms in which I found myself, I am hoping those storms will serve as lessons to many of you. Just know God can take the storms in your life and turn them into awesome blessings. Don't wait to be pushed into your purpose when God has already opened the door for you to walk through.

CHAPTER 1

WHAT HAS GOD CALLED YOU TO DO?

Has someone knocked on your door, and you waited before you answered? They came unannounced, so you were hesitant in your approach. Maybe fear kept you from answering the door, or maybe you just did not want to be bothered at the time. Eventually you answered, hoping what was on the other side was something that would be good for you, something that would not cause you any discomfort.

Well that is how God showed Himself to me. He knocked, I waited, and then I answered. Not only was something on the other side of the door, but it was so huge I had to share it with the world—it was Blessed 24:7®!

Blessed 24:7 was birthed out of a long struggle, but arrived right on time. Blessed 24:7 was God's way of testing and showing me that I must live each day knowing I was blessed 24:7, even in the middle of my storms. I know all too well and strongly believe that God does not put any more on us than we can handle. Jesus is the only reason I have been able to endure, survive, and thrive during times of stress and turmoil.

I own an on-line gift shop where I sell merchandise (gift items and apparel) imprinted with the phrase Blessed 24:7. The meaning behind the Blessed 24:7 phrase is a daily reminder for all that we are truly blessed by our creator 24 hours a day, 7 days a week!

The logo serves as an inspirational message to those who are seeking God's promise for their lives. I am the exclusive trademark owner of this now famous phrase, and God wanted me to share the Blessed 24:7 message with the world. However, before that, there first came a season of preparation. My faith was tested often.

Starting the Blessed 24:7 Gift Shop was a natural success for me after having what I thought was a successful career in the offices of corporate America. I also owned my own printing company, where I specialized in marketing and promotional products. I ran both of my businesses, the gift shop, and the printing company, part-time, while working my nine-to-five job. I started both of my companies from the ground up. I was able to accomplish this without a college degree and without formal training—now that is a blessing in itself. With the sale of Blessed 24:7 merchandise, I am able to share my amazing heartfelt message of struggle, vision, and God's promise with others. I want you to be spiritually motivated even when the storms of life come your way. The Blessed 24:7 message has been sent all over the world as a new way of thinking, feeling, and trusting during the rough times.

I have answered another knock, which is to take my ministry, the Blessed 24:7® Gift Shop, full time. This was the only direction I could have gone after being terminated from my corporate America job, where I spent 21 years of dedicated service.

Chapter 2

Trusting God in the
Middle of the Storm...

In a single year, I suffered many set backs, including the death of my stepfather, depression, and broken relationships with two of my life-long friends. This was just a few of the many dark places in which I found myself. While stuck in the middle of that storm, I was terminated from my job. It seemed like anything that could go wrong that year did go wrong.

Can you imagine being terminated from a job you spent 21 years going to every day? I gave them my very best, even when I felt like I was being treated unfairly. I left that job empty handed. I was denied unemployment benefits and was not offered a severance package. My faith was truly tested; I felt like the disciples when Jesus told them not to take anything for their journey. *Jesus said to them, "Take nothing for the way, neither staff, nor scrip, nor bread, nor money; nor to have two body-coats apiece" (Luke 9:3).*

5

To add insult to injury, I was terminated two days after my anniversary date. I planned to leave that job on my own one day, and I was sure I was going to have a fabulous retirement party, celebrating with all my colleagues with great gifts and well wishes.

Growing up, I was taught to be sure to seek employment at a company that could offer you job security and great benefits. We all know that in today's world, job security no longer exists.

Before being terminated from my job, God spoke directly to me, and He clearly gave me my assignment to run my ministry, Blessed 24:7, full time. I knew I was born to be an entrepreneur, but how could I when I was trapped inside my nine to five job? I was too afraid to step out on faith and, as a result, I slowly watched my dreams die as I sat inside my cubical at work each day.

The remaining years spent at my job became very unpleasant; I felt as if I was under attack, and the devil was far too busy. The atmosphere became so rough I often found myself praying on the way to work, praying in the parking garage, praying before entering the building, and praying on my way home.

There were times when I sat at my desk with tears in my eye. I knew I was in a place God had not intended for me to be. My season there had ended, but I stayed anyway. In spite of the many storms headed my way, I had to learn how to trust God, even in the middle of those storms. It's powerful when you trust, believe, and follow God. He has a special way of bringing you through the storms. God wants us to rejoice and celebrate Him even during the worst times of our lives. *Romans 5:2-3 says, "...and rejoice in hope of the glory of God. And not only so, but we glory in tribulations also."* God is telling us in His word to praise Him in the middle of our storms; know that God is always with you, before the storm, during the storm, and long after the storm!

CHAPTER 3

THE FAITH WALK— WHERE IS YOUR FAITH?

I was going to work every day too afraid to trust in what God had already promised me. I could not imagine leaving the job that was paying the bills and keeping a roof over my head and food on the table for both my son and me. In spite of the attack I was under, I still needed to provide for my family. I did not know how to do anything else but depend on my bi-weekly paycheck. You know, that was one of my biggest mistakes, pretending the job was the source of my survival, when indeed God was my source—the job was simply a resource.

How could I give up all those great company benefits, such as health insurance, stock options, paid vacation, and sick leave? I knew what God was calling me to do; I just did not know how to take that first step into my faith walk.

I love the Lord, I was going to church every

Sunday, and I was even sending my tithes to the storehouse. However, I was still not walking in my God-given purpose.

I was so afraid of being self-employed, afraid of not having enough money to cover my expenses. Self-employment meant no guarantees in your income and no paid sick days. How could I even dream of being self-employed? After all, I was a single parent with a teenage son who was about to graduate from high school and who plans to attend college. However, God was speaking to me, asking me, "Wanda, where is your faith?"

I began to feel like the disciples in the boat with Jesus during the storm. Just think, the disciples were already in the boat with Jesus, the One who has all power. The disciples had already seen Jesus perform miracles, but when the storm began to rock the boat, they became ·fearful. Jesus is the One whose voice can control the sea, the winds, and the water, yet they were still afraid. Jesus said to them, *"Where is your faith?" (Luke 8:25)*. The Lord was asking me the very same thing. The Word of God says in *John 20:29, "Blessed are they who have not seen and have believed."*

I should have been more like Simon, one of the fishermen; it is all about trusting God even when it does not make sense. Sometimes we have to step out on faith by going into the deep, leaving our comfort zone and entering the faith zone. We need to trust God on what He has called us to do.

Do you recall when the fishermen had been fishing all night and caught nothing? Keep in mind these were professional fisherman. They knew what they were doing and were very good at it. However, when Jesus was preaching at the lake and saw the fishermen, Jesus took note that they had been fishing and caught nothing.

In Luke 5:4-6, Jesus advised Simon to go out into the deep and let down his net. Simon pretty much told Jesus he had been at this all night and that there was nothing out there. It just did not make sense to Simon. However, Simon said, "At thy word I will let down the net," and when he did the fishermen enclosed a great multitude of fish—so many fish they broke the net. Simon trusted Jesus even when it did not make sense to do so. We should be more like Simon.

CHAPTER 4

WHEN FRIENDS AND FAMILY ABANDON YOU....

Just when I thought I had enough drama going on in my life, my friends—or shall we say so-called friends, and in some cases family, too—began to turn away. How could this be happening? I was doing no harm to anyone. I am saved, and I love the Lord with all my heart. I have turned my life over to Jesus; He is the Lord of my life! I know I am a daughter of the most high King, and I am truly Blessed 24:7.

What I did not know is that the friends in my circle refused to accept the changes I was allowing God to make in my life. I am talking about the changes that take place when one's relationship with God grows closer and stronger. My friends did not understand the change in me as I spent more time with the Lord in praise and worship. There is a major difference between knowing who God is and having a one-on-one relationship with the Master.

My circle of friends had been the same for the past 20 plus years. I had not made any changes to the company I had been keeping.

The people in my circle had some unacceptable worldly ways, and they did not take note that I was now walking in God's will, way, and His word. It appeared my friends could only remember when I used to party, hanging out at the club. The person who I thought was my very best (lifelong) friend turned against me. One of my requests to my friends was to stop cursing around me. I shared with my best friend how the cursing breaks my spirit, interrupts my closeness with Christ. It was my very best friend who reminded me that she could remember when I used to curse in the ninth grade.

I had these friends in my circle for far too long; I had no clue how to move them out of my circle. I did not want to appear to be uppity, too cute, and heaven forbid I did not want anyone to think I thought I was better than others in the circle. I simply made the mistake of keeping them in my circle and falsely assuming I could be their savior. Now imagine me trying to play Jesus the savior!

Surly my Christian walk could have been all the example they needed. Keeping these friends in my circle meant I had to make compromises with my environment. This particular environment did not give me the spiritual food for which I hungered.

It was obvious this friend was not going to accept my spiritual growth, and she had no idea that God was setting me up to be blessed. This friend later sent me a three- to four-page email cursing me out. She copied others on the email message she sent me. After sitting at my desk with tears rolling down my face, I could only reply letting her know I had no idea she felt this way. The email she sent me sounded as if she'd disliked me all her life and had never been my friend to begin with. I later told her I had done nothing but loved her like a sister. I went on to tell her that I would pray for her and love her like a sister but only from a distance. Well I said some others things (smile) but that was it.

Part of my storm was also my broken relationship with my teenage son, the son who I thought had just completely lost his mind. I am speaking about the child I raised as a single parent—the one for whom I made sacrifices. My son was now disrespecting and disobeying me!

I knew I had done nothing to warrant this behavior. I was a great mother who was in place at all times. I was home when he left for school, home when he returned. I attended every school meeting, did not miss a single field trip, and was the one who took him to soccer and basketball practice. I spend quality (one-on-one) time with him on weekend trips and several Caribbean cruises, just me bonding with my son and no other invited guests.

I was there for every high fever, stomachache, and loose tooth. I gave him my very best and all that was in me. I actually raised this child up in the church. He knew the Lord and accepted Jesus in his life at the age of seven. I thought I was the perfect picture of motherhood, but now I had to wonder where it all went wrong. I told God, whatever He has in store for me must be good because they say the bigger the storm the bigger the blessing.

CHAPTER 5

TAKING INVENTORY OF THE COMPANY YOU ARE KEEPING— GETTING RID OF THE DREAM KILLERS...

I was in a desperate search for a better relationship with my son. I also wanted to change the way my circle of friends appeared without causing hurt, harm, or shame. Before I could muster up the faith to get rid of the dream killers, God stepped in and handled it for me. The so-called friends that needed to be out of my circle ended up leaving on their own. They left in such an unsaved way, it left me with no desire to reconnect unless their lives were to change and they began to respect my walk with the Lord. The dream killers were now out of my life, and I pray for them often.

God was not going to bless me until I had taken complete inventory of the company I was keeping. God had a blessing just for me, and being the good steward that I am, God knew I would share my overflow of blessings with those in my circle. My overflow of blessings from God was sure to pour out on those who were in my circle, and closely connected to me. Guess what, when God has something for you, and your circle is not right (I am talking about when your house is out of order), God will hold your blessings.

God was not going to allow my overflow to spill on those who were not ready to handle such a blessing. The friends in my circle were not only dream killers but also blessing blockers. You know the kind of friends who stand in the way when God is trying to bless you.

Those friends are gone, and God has sent me some new ones. Now the relationship with my son . . . I am still waiting on that to get better. I have to remember that I ask God to use me as a vessel any way He sees fit. This means that sometimes when you go through something, it is *not* always about you. Remember you are now God's vessel, and when God needs to use you for somebody else's deliverance, He will. Be careful what you ask God for because He hears every prayer. I know all that is going on with my son is all about my son and the Savior, and I am the vessel caught in the middle.

God would not use me as a vessel and allow me to break without fixing me and lifting me up again. I pray for my son's deliverance, and I also know that what he is going through is about his own faith walk. I am already working on my next book titled, *The Season God Gave Me Back Everything the Devil Stole From Me.*

When it comes to your circle of friends, remember to align yourself with people who are equally yoked. Equally yoked is not just for the person you are marrying. Align yourself up with people who know how to worship, praise, and serve the Lord. Align yourself up with people who want something positive out of life, people who have dreams, visions, and are allowing God to use them for kingdom building.

You want to connect with others who have the desire to be elevated. You should be able to minister to those in your circle, and they should be able to minister to you. As you are lifted in His name, you are in a better position to be a witness to someone who does not know the Lord as you do. Take inventory of the company you keep as often as needed, a little winter and spring cleaning does the mind, body, and soul good.

It says in God's word to be mindful of the company you keep, for it can corrupt your mind. *Do not be misled: "Bad company corrupts good character" (1 Corinthians 15:33). "And if any man obey not our word by this epistle, note that man, and have no company with him, that he may be ashamed. Yet count him not as an enemy, but admonish him as a brother" (2 Thessalonians 3:14-15).*

CHAPTER 6

IS THAT YOU GOD? BECAUSE SOMETIMES SATAN TRIES TO GET A WORD IN...

There were many occasions where I felt I had been put in total isolation from the rest of the world. I was left on a deserted island all by myself. Friends and family could not see that I was answering the call of God, and that I was walking into my purpose, that place where all my passion existed. I could now see that I was walking in the favor of God.

Many of my friends and family members (dream killers) thought I was going overboard with my dream; my spirit of excellence was misunderstood. Some of my own family members did not take the time to understand what Blessed 24:7 was all about. They were not aware of the treasure that lay deep within my heart and soul.

I became confused about it all. Was God really

calling me into my purpose, or was this only what Wanda wanted? Before confusion (Satan) could even take over for one single second, God placed me in total isolation so I could have one-on-one time with Him. Remember, God is *not* an author of confusion.

The separation from friends and family actually allowed me to focus on what Jesus had been trying to tell me. During the isolation period, my faith was strengthening and my walk was now with confidence. I began to accept the isolation as a great place to be. I recalled Jesus Himself not being accepted in his own country and, went to other areas to preach the Word. *Luke 4:24 says, "No prophet is accepted in his own country." Mark 6:4 says, "But Jesus, said unto them, A prophet is not without honor, but in his own country, and among his own kin, and in his own house."*

My private time with God allowed Him to give me the gift of discernment, knowing the difference between when God is speaking to me versus when Satan is trying to sneak in a message. Let us not pretend the devil is not busy because you and I both know Satan is even busier when you are trying to be about your Father's business.

Do not be afraid for God to place you in isolation; do not be afraid to be on that island all by yourself. Your private time alone with God is

22

when He is able to deliver us from our fears and the things that are keeping us from allowing Him to use us as vessels for kingdom building. The private time with God is when you get your confirmation, where your dreams are unlocked, where the vision is clearly written in your heart.

To allow me to understand what my purpose was, God also sent certain people my way who were like angels of confirmation. One day I was volunteering at my son's former elementary school for career day, and a young lady sat next to me during a break. This was my first time ever meeting this woman, and we briefly talked about how the career day morning sessions were going.

Before the woman walked away, she told me she had a word for me from the Lord. This young lady had a scripture already written down on a small sheet of paper, which she shared with me. When I got home, I searched my Bible for the scripture and began to cry aloud after reading it. The scripture read, *"Blessed is she that has believed, for there shall be a fulfillment of the things spoken to her from the Lord" (Luke 1:45).*

This was my confirmation; this was the angel of confirmation sent by God. This was God speaking to me, letting me know that all I need to do is trust, believe in Him, and watch how He fulfills those things already spoken to me. This was just the beginning of my journey, and I still had a long way to go before I truly understood the bigger picture.

God continued to send people my way with some powerful messages. Church service on Sunday was always a word customized and exclusively designed for me—thank *you,* Pastor. I began to get more support from my immediate family, and they began to see the favor of God working in my life. My family's encouragement and support helped me to survive many of those storms.

CHAPTER 7

PUSHED INTO MY PURPOSE— MOVING FROM FEAR TO VICTORY...

Before being terminated from my job, I was on short-term disability for job-related issues that were stressing me out. I was being treated for depression. Imagine the Blessed 24:7 lady depressed! The depression was so overwhelming I found myself crying often. I literally cried for 130 days straight, and this was before I was terminated! During that 130-day cycle, God found many ways to speak to me.

I recall the day I was approved for the short-term disability leave. The night before the leave of absence from my job, I said a long and heartfelt prayer, crying out to the Lord to protect me from the enemy. I asked God to cover me, to hide me in the comfort of His arms. I prayed to God asking for confirmation for my purpose. I admitted to God that I was afraid, confused, and needed much guidance. I prayed for clarification and asked that any confusion be removed. That night I also said to the Lord, I would be more committed to reading His precious word daily and not just on Sundays or sporadically.

I told the Lord I would start each day with reading and mediating on His word. The next morning, the very first day of my leave and the night after I'd poured out my heart to the Lord, I opened up my Bible and you will not believe the scripture that was before my eyes. Now, keep in mind, this was the very first day of my official leave from my job; also keep in mind that God had already given me my assignment and I was just fearful of taking that leap of faith.

Here is what the scripture read: *"And it came to pass, when the king sat in his house, and the Lord had given him rest round about from all his enemies..." (2 Samuel 7).* Now, imagine how I felt when I read this on the same day I started my leave from my job!

It gets better, the other verse I read said, *"And Nathan said to the king, Go, do all that is in thine heart; for the Lord is with thee" (2 Samuel 7:3).* Now this was one of many confirmations from God to do what was in my heart and to trust because the Lord is with me. The other verse I read touched me as well: *"And I was with thee whithersoever thou wentest, and have cut off all thine enemies out of thy sight, and have made thee a great name, like unto the name of the great men that are in the earth" (2 Samuel 7:9).*

When I read "great name," you know I was thinking Blessed 24:7, that's the great name, a great name in the earth. The part about "cut off all thine enemies," well I felt like my former job was the enemy. In less than three months, after I was approved for the leave, while being treated for depression, while going through all the storms I mentioned, I was terminated from my job. I cannot begin to explain to you all the things that were going through my head. This could not be happening to me, not after 21 years on the job. I asked myself what does all this mean? Where do I go from here? Some say I was, "Pushed into My Purpose"!

Another year has gone by, and God is still keeping His promise. I simply consider my storms a test from God, a test that I was able to pass. These tests gave me an awesome testimony. We should always be willing to take any test God gives us. When you pass God's test, your blessing is released. God will take you to the next level in your ministry or walk with Him.

Just know you fail the test when you decide not to take it, and when you fail the test, your blessings are blocked. God needed me to be still so I could see all and hear all God was trying to reveal to me.

I was being set up by God, to be blessed! When God is ready to bless you, you must go through a process. You must be obedient to God's call, or you might miss your blessing. God has to know He can trust you with what He is about to release into your life.

When there is a special calling on your life, you have to be ready to move when God says move. Whatever you think you are lacking or missing for your journey, trust me, God will give you all you need. Sometimes you will not get what you need for the journey until you start the journey.

Keep this in mind: you do *not* have to be totally prepared when you are called by God to do something. Remember, He is God and through Jesus, you can do all things! I had to take my own phrase, "Blessed 24:7," and put it to use in my own life.

I truly understand what it means to be Blessed 24:7. God is with me at all times. He is with me before the storms, during the storms, and long after the storms. God blesses me 24 hours a day and seven days a week. God wants us to live each day knowing we are Blessed 24:7!

CHAPTER 8

PURSUING YOUR DREAMS

My life is a walking testimony, and God is not through with me yet. For the first time in my life, I'm a full-time business owner, the CEO/President of three companies (1) The Blessed 24:7 Gift Shop, (2) Printing Express & Designs, LLC and, (3) The Blessed 24:7 Foundation.

I started the third company, the Blessed 24:7 Foundation, so I could go into communities, schools, and churches to assist our youth and young adults with pursuing their dreams of becoming an entrepreneur. I teach a one-day seminar on "How to Start Your Own Business from Ground Zero."

I am also available to speak at conferences, sharing my amazing heartfelt story of struggle, vision, compromise, and God's promise. My goal is to motivate others to allow God to move them from fear to victory in pursuing their dreams.

The key to pursuing your dreams is obedience, being a good steward over the few things you have, and watching how God will bless you with much more. Being self-employed is no longer a thing I fear. You see, Jesus is my boss. He is the One who sees that I get my bills paid on time. Jesus has a benefits package no company can match, and Jesus can never fail. God has seen fit for me to stay on course, continue to dream, and bless others while my business ministry is growing.

Regardless of how dark the situation was, God blessed me in the middle of my storm. I was once a broken vessel, and now God has truly moved me from fear to victory. I am allowing God to use me in any way He sees fit. God can always enlighten your darkness. *Psalms 18:28 reads, "For thou will light my candle; the Lord my God will enlighten my darkness."*

Live your dreams. When you know it's God calling you, walk through the door that God has opened for you. Take back everything the devil stole from you and yes, reap the harvest God promised you! Yes, I was pushed into my purpose, and you can walk into yours!

The Blessed 24:7 Poem

I'm Blessed 24:7
God woke me up this morning,
And allowed me another day.
He let me go about my duties,
In his own very special way.
My whole life is much richer,
Without Him, I'd be so lost,
This is the life I chose to live
And I'll do it at any cost.
God will stand by me in all my endeavors
In everything, I attempt to do,
He'll show me the way when I'm lost,
All I need to do is be true.
I thank you God for everything,
For all the gifts from heaven.
I honor you and I praise you,
I know I'm Blessed 24:7. ©

Gladys Childs McCowin

Pushed Into My Purpose ™

How God moved me from fear to VICTORY!

READER'S TESTIMONIALS

I must inform you that I enjoyed your book, "Pushed Into My Purpose" tremendously. I read it three times and I plan to read it from time to time, whenever I need some spiritual uplifting. I had no idea that you went through all that you did and thank God that you survived it. The book is very well written and I am so proud of you. You continue to amaze me with your many talents, yet as your mother, I should not be surprised. Keep up the good work and I will see you on Oprah one day.

With much love, Your Mother –
Gladys Childs McCowin – Bowie, MD

My soul has been blessed since we first talked, but since reading the book, I am overwhelmed. My spirit jumped at the reading of every word, every page, and every chapter. I felt as if I had walked through your steps as my own as I read the book. I wholeheartedly understand the leading of you to write the book. I can relate so much to the book and know that your obedience to follow God's leading to write it is another confirmation on my purpose and having faith to step into God's calling. Continue to be a blessing to others and God's Favor will continue to flow on you and through you!

T. Carter, Events of Essence

"Pushed Into My Purpose" was a great book. This is a must read book for everyone. I can relate or have experienced everything you talk about in your book. God always allows you to meet people who can help you get through trials and tribulations that you are going through by reading what others have gone through before you. I had to read your book twice in one day because it was so good it helped me to see that God was really working on my behalf even though sometimes we doubt when we are going through things in our life. Thanks for taking the time to write your testimony it will truly be a blessing to a lot of people.

Amanda Showell – Orange, VA

Thank you so much for pursuing your dream and fulfilling your purpose. The book was well written; I enjoyed it being an easy, quick read. There are many gems for those seeking to do the will of God and ready to devote themselves to accomplishing God's purpose in their lives but there is a cost. Thanks for taking the time to point out the costs, the trials, and tribulations.

Blessings, Evangelist Evelyn Taylor

I just thank God for your humbleness, openness, and sincerity! Praise God for the victory. The book blessed me and ministered to "ME," can't wait to wear the shirt. Continue to be "REAL" and know that you are in our prayers!

Candy Rivers – Seattle, WA

First, I really enjoyed your book, "Pushed Into My Purpose." You are truly an inspirational woman with a lot of courage and a great entrepreneurial spirit. I just gave your book to my wife to read as well. She thoroughly enjoyed it as well.

Joseph M. Thornton, Jr. – Crofton, MD

Let me first congratulate you on walking into the purpose Jesus Christ has outlined for you. Your book was a blessing! I read the book last week while waiting for a flight to Louisville, KY. Let me tell you, I now understand why I have gone through many things I have experienced over the last year or so. I see now that was the beginning of my own journey. Looking forward to reading your next book!

Tracy Jones – Waldorf, MD

I loved your book, I thought that it was brief and to the point, EXCELLENT!!! To God be the glory....

Sandra Powell - Washington, DC

I took your book to the bowling alley with me this morning and read it in between my bowling turn. It was very interesting and spell binding. I just love the way you have at phrasing things. I finished the book before we left the bowling alley. God bless you and keep the faith. You are an encouragement to all and that is the way it should be.

Love you, Elvera

I wanted you to know that "Pushed Into My Purpose" came to me at just the right time. During this time of uncertainty and utter disappointment, I wonder if I have let my business down and not the other way around. God gave me the vision I am sure and I hope that I can do the things that I have to do to make the dream a reality. Thanks for the encouragement.

Joe Elliott – Petersburg, VA

Your book was awesome. It really confirmed for me that I am truly on my path to my purpose. There were so many things that you said that let me know that this is where I am suppose to be. So many other things I could relate to even with the child situation. I must tell you this, the BEST is yet to come and just know this, and God has not forgotten you.

God Bless, Patricia

Sister- I already felt the anointing when I opened it and started to read- it is powerful; you are blessed! Thanks again - Stay Encouraged!!!

Marian Newman Braxton - Winchester, VA

Wanda, the book arrived yesterday! I was so excited....I sat on my bed and IMMEDIATELY read if from cover to cover. I really enjoyed the book and can relate to a lot of what you said. I always enjoy hearing testimonies of God's work. I truly believe that, with God, ANYTHING is possible. I wish you continued success and I look forward to your next book.

Much Love, Sharone - Louisa, VA

Hi Wanda, I met you at the gallery when Michael Basin had the networking gathering. I really enjoyed your book I got up in the middle of the night around 3:00am and could not put it down. I keep it with me at all times just to stay focused on my goals. I am the future talk show host that you met. One of my co-workers read your book he enjoyed it. He said he was going to order some products.

Thanks, Michelle Griffin – Rockville, MD

Hello Wanda, both mom and I have read "Pushed Into My Purpose" and found it to be very inspiring. I am sure that all of your readers will walk by faith and not by sight as we continue and seek our purpose in life.

Be Blessed & Much Love,
Arnold - Richmond, VA

Printed in the United States
202117BV00001B/55-303/P